A CELEBRATION OF ELTHAM IN VERSE

Layout and Design by Andy Grachuk © 2013
www.JingotheCat.com

DEDICATED TO ELTHAM POETS

PAST, PRESENT AND FUTURE.

CONTENTS

Celebrate Eltham today

FORWARD

The poet Andrew Motion reminded us in his anthology of poetry *Here to Eternity* how every child wants to know 'Who am I?' and 'Where am I?' One can often hear them spinning out their addresses: name, house, town, city, country, hemisphere, ending with 'the world, the universe, space!' Motion calls this game a folk ritual which reflects everyone's need to know and understand themselves and where they live. This need never leaves us and poetry has a place in helping us to answer these questions.

My work in the School of Education at the University of Greenwich involves teaching and researching about how English and literacy is and can be taught. I love teaching about poetry and demonstrating how poetry really matters. Many will argue that poetry matters first to the writer and then to the reader and is able to deal in a unique way with important subjects for those writing it. Poetry can often explore everyday reality, showing it in a new and revelatory light. Through the process of writing poetry people can discover things about themselves and their environment. So, I was delighted when Gaynor Wingham asked me and my colleagues Gordon Ade-Ojo and Amanda Henshall to be involved in a project to encourage people to write poems about Eltham.

Judging poetry in a competition is never easy. As I have said, poems often matter more to the writer than to the reader. We all read poems using our own experiences and our own beliefs about what a poem can be and what it can do. However, all three of us were looking for work that exploited what poetry can offer in terms of tone, sounds, voices, forms, patterns and rhythms.

The judging panel were moved by the number of poems that were submitted that demonstrated people's passion and love for their town. Not all of the poems were uncritical, but all celebrated the people, places and cultures that make Eltham what it is today.

It was a privilege to be involved in this project and to be given the opportunity to read the poems from the people of Eltham.

Professor Andrew Lambirth June 2013

University of Greenwich

Faculty of Education and Health

INTRODUCTION

Eltham, our Eltham, is a South East London suburb in the Royal Borough of Greenwich with a diverse multi cultural population of about 80,000. It is an area rich in history, a generous amount of parks and woodland and a busy High Street. But could Eltham be a source of inspiration for poetry?

We have had our poets before in Eltham and some immortalisation in verse. Edith Nesbit, famous author of The Railway Children, lived at Well Hall, Eltham for a number of years and wrote many poems. Eltham is mentioned several times by Shakespeare and also by Chaucer. However, could twenty first century people write poetry about Eltham? In 2013 many adults and children, took up this challenge to Celebrate Eltham in Verse and were enthusiastic to explore this art form to tell the world about Eltham .. their Eltham.

This book draws together a selection of the poems submitted by adults and children for this community poetry competition, organised by Eltham Town Centre Partnership, a group of local stakeholders in the town. It was judged by a panel from Greenwich University and the celebratory event and prize giving was a great success. It was very difficult to select winners and select poems to include in this book. The book hopefully reflects the range of poems and subjects submitted by people who live, have lived, work, shop or go to school here.

The poems show that Eltham has a lot to celebrate. It has an astonishing history stretching back many centuries . Henry V11's children lived here at a Royal Palace in Eltham in the 15th century , and the Courtauld family incorporated original palace buildings into an Art Deco gem in the 1930's . Eltham Palace, now run by English Heritage, is mentioned in many poems. Poetry has certainly been written at Eltham Palace. In 1499 it is recorded that the child Prince Henry (later Henry V111) challenged the famous Dutch scholar and philosopher Erasmus, to write a poem. Within 3 days of being challenged, Erasmus had written a poem praising England, King Henry VII and the two princes, Arthur and Henry.

Not far from Eltham Palace there is a magnificent sixteenth century building, now called the Tudor Barn and a restaurant, which was built for Sir Thomas Moore's daughter Margaret Roper. This building is set in lovely parkland, the Pleasaunce , which delights many visitors. Edith Nesbit lived in a house next to the Tudor Barn in the 20c.

Even earlier than both of these the Romans marched through the area and archeologists have discovered they settled here too.

We have our University in Eltham. Avery Hill, once a woman's teacher training college established in 1906 in the former home of Colonel North, how houses a number of Greenwich University departments and has a student Halls of Residence in the grounds.

The many famous people who have been born or lived in Eltham are mentioned by a number of our poets. One of our famous sons is the actor Bob Hope who was born here in 1902 , later moving to the USA, and is commemorated appropriately in the name of our local Bob Hope Theatre.

The poems describe more recent life in Eltham. In the 20th century the area changed from a small village to a thriving town. There are poems which nostalgically look back at times past and childhoods days . One poet describes the history of her family who arrived from Ireland several generations ago. My own family mirrors this experience. We came and stayed. Eltham continues to welcome newcomers , and embraces families, old and new, who choose to settle here, contributing and enjoying local life.

Eltham is proud of its parks and woodlands. Oxleas Woods, Eltham Park, Avery Hill, Queencroft Park, the Pleasaunce and the Tarn are all celebrated in the poems. Children and adults clearly love and appreciate time spent in the open air and the wildlife which is all around us. We even welcome wildlife newcomers to the area , our green parakeets are the subject of a delightful little poem.

Our Town Centre with its mix of shops, restaurants, banks and community meeting places has had its challenges over the years, but remains vibrant and a focal point for the town. Poems reflect the importance that the Town Centre has for everyday life in Eltham. Children and adults write with passion and humour about the High Street, whether they shop , eat or pound the beat as a local copper.

Eltham has had its difficulties as well as its good times. Life can be hard for some people. The winning poem by ten year old Jack Powell mentions giving money to a homeless man and another reflects on 'Unlucky Eltham'. The street riots in the Summer of 2011 frightened children and adults alike and made people realise that , although life can be pleasant here, we live in an urban area and there can be tensions.

What comes through the poems is that Eltham is important to people's lives. It is part of London, part of Royal Greenwich (of which people are proud) , but Eltham is Eltham. It is definitely Eltham. What is inspiring is the enthusiasm of our children who enjoy going to school, playing in the parks, going to the Town Centre , know its history, but see it and love it as it is . Reading these must give us hope that our future is in safe hands.

Our Eltham poems have been written by children and adults who have spoken from their hearts about Eltham and what it means to them. We hope you enjoy them .

Gaynor Wingham
Eltham Town Centre Partnership Arts Rep
June 2013

Photos with kind permission from

John King, Richard Cains, Gaynor Wingham, Mike Robinson, Jean Lendon, and John Webb

Thank you to our sponsors and supporters of 'Celebrate Eltham In Verse Competition', including

Greenwich University, McDonalds, The Eltham Society, Eltham Park Residents Association, Normans Music, Total Beauty, The Casket, Metropolitan Police, This is Eltham website , The Eltham Centre, St Mary's Centre , Eltham Churches, English Heritage and SEnine magazine.

A special thank you to Michael Kelpie who made this book possible.

All authors retain copyright of their poems and photos.

Avery Hill Blossom - Richard Cains

Memories of Eltham Past

I USED TO GO TO ELTHAM

I used to go to Eltham.
Legs sticking to hot vinyl seats
in the back of a bus-red Cortina
that Dad's mate sprayed
in Plumstead Depot
when the foreman wasn't in.

I used to go to Eltham.
'round to my uncle's flat.
My aunt's whisky-laugh through the door
and when it opened
the smoke didn't matter
cos her smile went up to her eyes.

I used to go to Eltham.
Ten bags and Mum's white fingers
catching my aunt's tea-break at M&S.
Everyone and everything she knew,
he's dead, she's left, they're back on.
A whole town in ten minutes.

I used to go to Eltham
Still do here and there.
My family's gone and the old shops too.
But you need a bit of rain,
she used to say.
That's why her smile went up to her eyes.

by Scott Landers

This poem was awarded 1st Prize in the adults category. Judges comments:

"*It is a poem about memories of Eltham and family life. The poet uses unusual language to evoke images of an old Eltham and there is a story in every verse, full of characters, times and events. There is joy and delight and a hint of sadness in those lines. The whole poem conjures up a terrific atmosphere of nostalgia and the panel were very impressed with how the poet had crafted this poem.*"

LIVING ACROSS FROM QUEENSCROFT PARK

Living across from Queenscroft Park,
I played with my friends until it got dark.
We played 40-40 and hide and seek,
Every day and every week.

We lived over the park, every day and night,
In the Summer, it was the height
Of all our lives, all down the street,
It was the place where we'd always meet.
I went back as a grown up and wanted to see,
The Old Faithful, the old mangly tree,
I climbed it dozens, up to the top,
Whilst my parents yelled at me to stop.

The memories of Queenscroft Park do make me smile
And although it has been a long while
I will never forget the memories it gave me
In fact, its ever after and most Happily!!!

We had the paddling pool and play park,
The skating rink where we would lark.
I remember Old Bert with his trunk full of skates,
And sometimes we climbed over the locked gates.

The park was my life when I was a kid,
And I wish I could go back and relive the things I did.
Between the two greens was a great community
Popping in and out of houses drinking cups of tea.

I loved playing rounders until it got too dark to see
With all of the neighbours, there was rivalry.
The park keepers were exceedingly glum,
But when the park closed, they became fun.

by Kala Whyte

*Kala Whyte spent her childhood in Middle Park and now in her 30's recalls happy
memories of the local Queencroft Park.*

GORDON SCHOOL

Gordon School
Apprehension was the feeling I felt
As I walked through the entrance gate
First day at a new school
(One entrance for boys and one for girls)
As I looked up at this building in awe
Well I'm here for 3 years more
Here I learnt about French, Geography and History
In classrooms that were cold and draughty
Built in 1904 this beautiful building
Still stands proud as it ought.

by Irene Brown

ELTHAM HIGH STREET

High Street where once in peace could walk
One battles today to find some space
Buses more than ever before
Now travel up and down
in groups of two or more
Cinemas have all but gone
It's new Hi Tec and Low Tec mobile phones
And trying to dodge buggies electric scooters and people's feet
It is becoming quite a feat
It's all for one and one for no one
I suppose progress goes that way

By Irene Brown

Irene, now in her 70's, moved to Eltham as a child after WW2 and attended Gordon School. She now lives in Phlipots Almhouses, just off Eltham High Street.

Seeing Philipots for the First Time

Standing at the wooden gate
Looking across the lawn
At the garden opposite
Awash with flowers
Yellow Mullen stalks weaving in the breeze
Rain drops shining on the leaves
Bluetits squabbling
Blackbirds chasing each other across the lawn
At speed
People I don't know chatting on the footpath
Exchanging gossip
The distant sound of the traffic
Disjointed voices
From the other side of the wall
A quiet and peaceful atmosphere
The realization
I could work here
I could live here
A quiet feeling that I would

By Sharon Staples

Sharon Staples is the Warden of Philipots Almshouses which was established in the 17th century in Eltham. She came to Eltham in 1983 and stayed. A wonderful resource for older Eltham residents with a lovely garden.

Remembering Eltham

Remembering Eltham
Electricity everywhere
London location
Historic houses
Amiable acquaintances
My Eltham home place

Everywhere I went
Lingering loving
Thoughts towards
Home happily
Always accompanied
Me. Travels now memories

by Margaret Taylor

Margaret remembered Eltham with affection from her travels in times past.

My Days In Eltham

I was born in Eltham and
Spent my childhood years
Enjoying my life through
laughter and tears

We played as kids at
the back of the palace
We climbed up the trees
with no damage or malice

There was an old tramp
with a broken down bike
Who trundled around
who everyone liked

We gave him our pocket money
to buy himself food
Children were nice then
not spiteful and rude

We loved living in Eltham
with the fields and the park
We had lots of fun days
and many good laughs

But all good things
must come to an end
I grew up and got married
had two children to tend

But now I am old
I think of the past
On my wonderful childhood
that just went so fast

by Maureen Sanderson

Maureen Sanderson (Nee Cope) now lives locally in Plumstead and is approaching 80. She recalls fondly her childhood days before and after WW2 in Eltham .

THE LOST LIDO ELTHAM PARK 1985

After school in the open air pool
The breeze is warm but the water cool
The sun is bright, still high in the sky
The concrete is hot where our towels dry

It will be home time soon, time for tea
But the kids are shouting dad, dad an ice cream for me
But no , no we have to go
I have to make the tea and you have homework to do,

But if tomorrow the sun is bright, and I can get away
Then we will all be back at the end of the day
Where the breeze is warm and the water's cool
In our very own open air pool.

by John Wingham

Dip into the Past

No towels tell where the youngsters are bound,
no lifeguards hover, no shrill whistles sound.

No no-bombing notice, no 'times up' to flout,
no children's teeth chatter to signal get out.

No fingers glow with renewed circulation,
no slopes run down to the quieter station.

Despite the campaign to restore her, named SPLASH
the old lady perished from shortage of cash.

Where Fido frolics beside the bypass
the lido lies buried beneath the cut grass.

by Geoff Lander

Eltham Lido was opened in 1924 in Eltham Park . It was a great source of enjoyment to several generations , but sadly was closed in 1988 and the area is now grassed over.

AND SNIFTERS IN THE CAB

Drink is destructive, drink is a curse,
most like a driver to be risk averse,
but tipsy's diverting, sobriety's drab,
the odd little snifter can brighten the cab.
The law suggests dozing day-trippers deserve
a sober approach to the London bound curve.
Few are aware of the crew's light and bitters,
some like the speed, save one, who has jitters--
as Eltham Park passes, the desperate guard,
fearing catastrophe blips the brakes hard.
His warning's too late! The bogey wheels screech!
Tragedy ruins a day at the beach.

By Geoff Lander

At 21.35 on 11/06/72 at Well Hall , Eltham there was a tragic train crash. Six people died, and 126 were injured. The public enquiry found evidence that the driver was intoxicated

WEDDING AT ELTHAM CHURCH

The rain lashed down.
Guests dripped over pews

And bridesmaids brushed mud from their shoes

The bride's mother squelched up the aisle.
The usher tried not to smile
As the feathers drooped on her hat.

But then the bells rang out
And a patch of light
Touched the bride and groom.

Raindrops sparkled and danced.
All was well
At the wedding at Eltham Church

by Sue Williamson

The Parish Church of St John's stands at the centre of Eltham High Street. With a history going back over 900 years the church has seen many weddings , some in the rain!

Timeline

I see Eltham through my Grandfather's eyes,
Through the childhood stories and family ties
In 1910, the Clarks rolled over the Irish Sea
Edward, my Grandfather, the youngest of these
Roper Street the home where the 3 boys shared a bed,
Eating their weekly treat of dripping and bread.

Their school no-one could believe was only the next door,
As always late and last through the gate they tore.
Eltham park, the bridge where as the smallest he,
Would be hung upside down, to dangle and scream
His sister would come to save him at his cries,
Scolding his brothers and marching them home pulled by their ties.

The three brothers only just grow then sent off to war,
One soldier, one sailor, my Grandfather the air core
One night returning to sirens sounding,
He shot down to the bomb shelter his heart pounding,
To the shock of his life, his was all on his own
His race back out, not thinking of his safety alone

Where could they be? He hunted through, gardens and sheds.
All through the house and under the beds
He ran down the high street and soon came to a stop,
As he saw a candle of light, but not from a shop
For in the Rising Sun he found his kin,
Having a stout and mother a gin

His gran called him over to say 'Well, if to die, be it a happy place'
In her thick Irish accent & big smile on her face!
The war came to an end, they all married but one,
Losing his dear sister, far too young
Like the high street itself, their lives changed pretty fast
From late 40's, the years soon past.

My Grandmother decided to show how far they had come
To add an 'e' to Clark, where before they had none.
My mother was born and knew nothing of this change
Until later she noted all the different spellings on certificates and thought it so strange
30yrs years on I, their first grandchild born,
My grandfather gift, rose coloured glasses for me to be worn

He took me to such a wonderland place,
Where golden eagles came to life from palace gates,
Where shop keepers once knew everyone by name
And my Grandfather's win at school had made the wall of fame.
I still look back fondly at places where once I played,
In the Pleasaunce Gardens, where giant snowmen where made

Years again on now, I fell in love all over again
Feeling so close to my Grandfather and where he began.
I bought I little flat, which is not much to most,
But with a bit of work I now believe I can boast
I enjoy the beauty that most don't get to see
Eltham, this great little place so special to me

I now welcome my daughter to soak up the past and embrace the new
I tell her stories of my own and about the area she belongs too
And how now it's the Royal Borough of Greenwich no less,
Oh how my Grandfather would laugh and call her, your highness
Though Eltham has changed over time in so many ways,
It's not just a town, its memories, our home, where I plan to stay

By Alex Farrow.

Five generations of Alex Farrow's family have lived in Eltham This great poem shares family memories shows how firm the roots are for many Eltham families.

EALTHAM OLD TOWN NEW ZEALAND

Ealtham - old town
on the track
north and south.........

Settlers came
shaped you out of
bush and swamp.
A town of firsts
roads, lamplight, dairy
butchers, bakers and grocery stores
busy, bustling charm.

Years go by
and all that changed
city drift
empty shops.
You had to reinvent
now crafts, coffee and bric a brac
still busy, bustling charm.

Eltham - my town
on the road
north and south.

by Maree Liddington

People have travelled all over the world from Eltham, taking the name of their town with them . This poem was submitted from Eltham in New Zealand , which is said to be named after our Eltham in London. It celebrates pride in their town and history.

Well Hall Pleasaunce - Mike Robinson

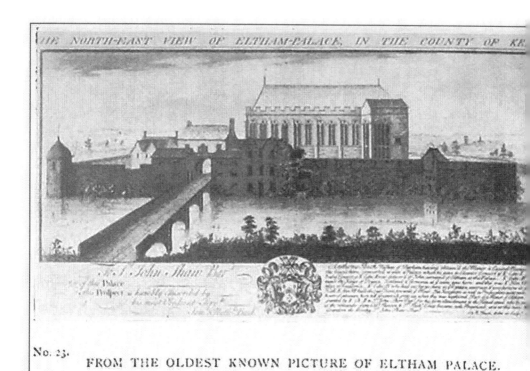

No. 23.

FROM THE OLDEST KNOWN PICTURE OF ELTHAM PALACE.

(Engraved by S. & N. Buck. 1735).

1735 - Picture of Eltham Palace

1915 - The Tarn, Eltham

AVERY HILL COLLEGE, ELTHAM—WINTER.

Avery Hill College, early post card. Now Greenwich University

Early 1900's , Avery Hill Park

ELTHAM'S MAGNIFICENT HISTORY

Henry V111 Once Rode

Henry VIII once rode from Palace and far
A vital part played in many a war
Munition workers and shipbuilders too
Famous writers and comedians to name but a few
Endless history and beauty for all to see
Eltham's history is there and still meant to be

by Dana Wiffen

From Miles of Farmland

From miles of farmland and dirt tracks for roads
Along came the railways then trams, then homes
As the population grew the open land disappeared
They built & built and more homes appeared
Now like many towns in London it's overpopulated, overbuilt and overgrown
But with history so rich who wants to go

by Dana Wiffen

These two short poems encapsulate the changes and history from royalty, to housing munition workers from the Woolwich Arsenal and more housing developments, The farmland is now built over , but the history remains and is remembered.

PROUD ELTHAM

Proud Eltham, past obscured in time
Lies close to famous London town.
Yet here we've cause for pride as well
Should we take time to seek and tell.

Let's offer hands across the years,
To those whose story played before.
Good people dwelt here, tilled the soil
Led peaceful, rural lives, but poor.
Long lost to us in mist of time,
They lived and toiled nearby my door.

Six hundred years our Palace stood,
Built large beside the farmers' lanes
Presiding o'er those fields of yore
As shepherd, sheep, looked up in awe.
And still that Great Hall stands up proud
Reminds us of the royal power.
Queens, kings and princes here before,
Did ride these parks to hunt. They saw
A world now lost, so rich, no more.

In Pleasaunce Gardens, fragrance rare,
Were Tudor ladies strolling there?
Escaped from London's foul-breathed lair
Down here to countryside so fair.
Kings' relaxation, sweet fresh air
Bequeathed such heritage of care.

Great River Thames, runs down nearby,
Her waters deep like history flow.
We'll tell the tales of heroes lives,
But truth to say, beneath the waves
Dark deeds of villains also lie.
Once Greenwich was mere settlement.
As river's bounty people sought.
The Saxons lived here. Romans fought,
And Viking raids disorder brought.

Since then did Eltham slowly grow,
And those past days left much to know,
Of 'Grenewic' shire in which we dwell.

So many kings loved Eltham well
And gracious Queens were holding court
'Tween palaces in these fair parts.
And with them came the great and good
To foster science, thought and arts.

They've marked our card of history well.
Meridian, unique on earth,
Bears witness o'er the world at large
To great men's visions counting time,
And finding stars to light men's way
Not drifting lost in oceans vast
As folk were lost in days gone past.

Imagination, inspiration,
'The Age of Reason' known to us,
When thinking men investigated,
Solved great problems, innovated.
Legacies for life's safe passage
Running threads thro' lives right now.
So fruitful, left their treasures vast,
Such wisdom down the years they cast.

But what of ordinary men?
For peasants then were folk as you
Lived out their days in Eltham too.
Their tales of travails, hopes and fears
Are told in legend o'er the years.
Dismiss not deeds of days afar
Those happenings tell us who we are.

Not far from here the pilgrims walked
Their weary way to Becket's door.
And Shooters Hill, once Watling Street,
Was prowled by highwaymen, for sure.
And know Wat Tyler trod Blackheath
Inspiring men demanding more.

Take pride good people, be of cheer,
Ancestors lived and loved right here.
This Eltham which we all hold dear,
Familiar to us, also theirs.
Men, women, children, all have seen,
Same river, palace, park so green,

Each generation has its day
And memory of us will leave
A stitch in history's complex weave.
Our years unfurl, but links in chain!
Not one will pass this way again!
So offer hands across the years,
To those before, and those un-born
Who'd share our pride in Eltham.

By Tessa Cheek

Tessa Cheek's poem gives a wonderful account of the pride that people have in Eltham and its history .

ELTHAM

A place of history
Where kings and queens played
in palaces and parks, overlooking
the winding Thames.
A hilly, spacious place with
deer and wild pigs.
A place with a view.
Now, a modern town,
shops, sports centre, houses, flats,
library, parks.
A place where families and
individuals can grow and develop.
A large community
Touched and nourished by history.
It still has a view.

by Patricia Duffy

Eltham's history is all around the modern town and touches lives today

Eltham Regis

When deer ranged wild in Eltham's park lands,
Mighty oaks grew thick on Kentish Downs,
Our monarchs used to come and hold their revels
In ancient halls within the Palace bounds.
Sunlit were the days of Eltham's glory,
When courtiers filled the Palace with their play,
And townsfolk came to watch the archers shoot
On lands that still bear linking names today.
Those days have gone, the Royal ties were broken,
And with them went the pageantry and fame;
But now The Queen has blazed our glory —
And Eltham shares the Borough's 'Royal' name.

by Ken Timbers

Royal Eltham old and new is celebrated as part of Royal Greenwich .

ELTHAM PALACE

Feeling bored, young Prince Henry
Stared up at the magnificent Hammerbeam ceiling
Wondering if he could get out of the meeting
With Erasmus

Henry coveted the scroll clutched by Arthur
Knowing this would curry favour with the great
Scholar. He had nothing to present but decided
To shine in his own way.

Later Erasmus commented that Henry showed a
Royal demeanour, a dignity of mind and remarkable
Courtesy. A pervasive charm bestowed upon....

Catherine of Aragon – Divorced
Ann Boleyn – Executed
Jane Seymour – Died
Anne of Cleeves – Divorced
Kathryn Howard – Executed
Only Katherine Parr had the last laugh – widowed
At least she kept her head

by Doreen Thorogood

*The Palace and Henry V111 are iconic in Eltham. The philosopher Erasmus came to
Eltham and may have influenced the history of England from his time in Eltham Palace
with the young Henry.*

Eltham Palace

In yesteryear, in days of yore
There stood a palace true and pure
Where household Royal
And servants loyal
Ruled the realm and upheld law.

Where banners waved and pennants flew
Jousts were met and trumpets blew
Whence mead was had
And folks were glad
Knights were brave and bold and true.

The lands for furlongs stretched around
And wild game was oft abound,
Feasts were ate
And full was plate
The revelry for Kings astound.

But faded now these days are gone
In distant past as time moves on
Yet cast aside
The palace hides
In barn disguise, now lost, forlorn.

Now buried beneath earth of brown
By wind and rain twas beaten down
Its patrons dead
No tears shed
For ruined palace and vanished crown.

Then resurrected from the grave
In decade new, the palace saved
In glory splendid
Two styles blended
Art-Deco mansion bold and brave.

And drinks were poured and music played
Smokers smoked and swingers swayed
A dream pursued
Palace renewed
And from history will never fade.

But war did come and bombs rained down
And devastated London town
Palace alight
But damage slight
And hampered not the sites renown.

The residents away then went
To warmer climes with warm intent
Replaced by ranks
With Army's thanks
To educate to great extent.

And finally to present times,
The grandeur of this place so fine
One and All can come to see
This marvel of our history
Its legacy is yours and mine.

A new breed of Palace Guard
Custodians and modern bards,
Instead of holding sword and shield
Its history and past we wield
Our Eltham held in high regard.

By Larry Bennett

Eltham Palace is now run by English Heritage . This poem gives a colourful account of the history from a Royal Palace, abandonment, rebuilding by the Courtauld family , the WW2 bombs, occupation by the Army, and now a lovingly restored building and grounds open to the public.

2012 Eltham High Street - Gaynor Wingham

Eltham Palace Bridge - Mike Robinson

Eltham Park - Gaynor Wingham

Well Hall Pleasaunce - Richard Cains

Reflections on Nature, Parks and Woodland

ANCIENT OXLEAS WOODS

For forty thousand years it stood
In ancient landscape: Oxleas Wood.
Before the skill of cultivation
Scrawny children faced starvation
And stalked the deer, the stag, the boar
Blood stains on the forest floor.
The annual snowfall's harsh arrival
Makes a battle of survival.
A strangled rabbit, tethered hare
Gave them that day their daily fare.

For forty thousand years it stood
The sacred hillside: Oxleas Wood.
Archaeologists have found
A pagan altar in the ground
A great stone table rests on rocks
Made for the springtime equinox.
On the stonework there are signs
(Concentric circles, random lines) –
The experts shake their heads and say
The Ancients cursed the motorway.

For forty thousand years it stood
Green and pleasant: Oxleas Wood.
Hear the humble pigeon cry,
As English history passes by.
No Roman legion, heartless Danes
No Norman conquest trace remains
The British Empire needed trees
For wooden boats to rule the seas.
Trees for homesteads, kindling, fuel
The age-ring marks the spring renewal

By Mary Dixon

The ancient Oxleas woodland , which stretches back 40000 years, covers many acres and includes rare plants and trees. It has a long history of use as wonderfully described in this poem . It is currently a place where dogs are walked, children ride their bikes and everyone enjoys the changing seasons and wildlife .

PLEASAUNCE MIDWINTER

The sky is clear, the moon so bright
I walked in an Eltham winter night
The air cold, bracing, biting face
Hands thrust deep in pockets, head low
I continue down Well Hall Road

Metal fence barricades the Pleasaunce Park
Near leafless trees howling into the dark
Branches reaching high skyward praying
Homage to the land, the moat and the barn
Silent witness of those past seeking calm

A late squirrel scampers across the path
Past the now frozen fountain bird bath
Squirrel stops, a statue, a fox on the prowl
Aloof proudly making his own lonely way
I call, he stares not running or afraid

From a shadow I notice something move
Flaxen hair flowing, skin sallow smooth
Squirrel runs to her the fox looks in distain
I stare mesmerised not believing the sight
Of this apparition on the winter drab night

Not floating or walking she moves in a glide
Hair gently bouncing, eyes open wide
Chiding the fox as he slowly moves away
Her eyes turn to me, clear and bright
Step back, not in fear, caught in her sight

Trees bend gently and whisper a song
With the wind, the branches sing along
I strain to hear words fleeting, calming
She looks toward me, eyes glimmering
An aura surrounds bright and shimmering.

Moonbeams break clouds, glancing and dancing
Lighting her form, delicately enchanting
I walk toward her into the Pleasaunce
Drawn, transfixed, toward her magic light
Needing, wanting to remain in her sight

Closer and closer, fainter she grows
Running along Eltham's ancient hedge rows
Now where she stood, I stand, alone
Under tree, the squirrel, fox and I
A lock of hair drops from the sky

Straining, in the moon night dark
I reach for it in night so stark
In hand, first shimmering in moonlight
The flaxen hair lock grows quickly duller
To a leaf, gold brown in winters colour

The wind in the trees whisper to me
They hold a message, what can it be
I concentrate to hear what is said
A message so fleeting, quiet and kind
I strain with eye, ear and mind

A friend, happy spirit, contented one
Wandering Earth, Sea and Sky following the sun
Not wanting, seeking or needing at all
Trees whisper a name, I smile at my stager
Witnessed the presence of Mother Nature

The sky now clear, the moon so bright
I walked in this Eltham midwinter night
The air cold, refreshing and clean
Contented at this turn of fate
Meandering home in the Eltham night late.

By Mark Wall

EXPECTATION

I wander around the Pleasaunce
Now winter is at close
The bare brown stoney earth is hard
I pass a redundant hose
These daylight hours are precious
So few in these short days
But tiny shoots of green are seen
They grab at days last rays

Could this on be a snowdrop
The first sweet flower to show
And bare its delicate white and green
As they bravely push through the snow

Just below earth's surface
There lies a wondrous scene
Roots and shoots of every sort
Will soon be showing green

I've notices these past mornings
The birds begin to sing
I see the Pleasaunce crocuses
I realize it's Spring.

By Josie Byfield

The area which is now Well Hall Pleasaunce dates back many hundreds of years . The house for Margaret Roper, now the Tudor Barn , was built in the 16c and nearby the house later occupied by Edith Nesbit was built in the 18c. The park was opened to the public in 1933 and is a beautiful area of flower gardens and less formal areas with a diverse wildlife.

Evening in Eltham Park

The dark woods tipped bronze
by the last rays
of an October sun.

Unseen cars a constant thrum,
and between the traffic's noise,
the wet green of grass
and the dark woods tipped bronze,
a swing in the playground
lurching backwards, forward, then back again.

An eccentric parabola,
backwards, forwards
and no-one in sight.

By Geoff Carlyle

The Eltham Parakeets

What is the best way to greet
The Eltham Park green parakeet?
Should you holler or squawk
Should you sing, scream or talk?
Perhaps you should send them a tweet

By Mary Dixon

Eltham Park is a large grassy area with a children's play area, tennis courts and a popular recreational area for people in Eltham. There are lovely trees along the pathways. The park is in two sections - North and South - divided by a road and railway line.

THE TARN

The Heron glides in on lazy wings.
He dips his beak and forms perfect rings.
Each time he wins. Sated, away his swings.

Then a moorhen gathers her little brood.
As they bob away in search of food.
Restless, she clucks in a gentle mood.
Near the bridge I linger charmed by my treasured Green Flag Park.

The morning rays sparkle on the lake.
High Clouds drift as birds awake.
Eager blackbirds sings "Time to wake".

Trees murmur gently while they sway.
As herons fly in after break of day.
Robins chirp, feisty and gay.
Now the wildlife starts their day.

by Jane Chandley

The Tarn is a small park which takes its name from the lake which is a remnant of the late C17th grounds of Eltham Lodge which was once within the Great Park of Eltham Palace . It is a haven for wildlife which is celebrated in this poem.

IN ST JOHN'S CHURCHYARD

Sunrise in October, 7.52a.m
The tombstones in St John's churchyard
are now verdigris, now neon green;
slashed by charcoal shadows, Names,
obscured by the grind of weathers,
are lost in time and memory.
7.53, the 321 hauls up Eltham Hill.
The stones are impassive
to the traffic, to the sun,
To the low light that paints tonal geometries
across the granite.
Names and dates carry no poignancy now,
faded so long, their substance is ghost,
who held them precious who
danced and sang and dreamt with them,
who pledged love in darkened rooms
on some cold morning stood here -
their lives, too, a short dream.
Autumn leaves pepper the ground.
Inside the church, a transient light
smears the walls;
outside, skeletal trees whisper of
how nothing ends, how everything ends,
time and time again

by Geoff Carlyle

St John's churchyard with its tombstones is an area of peace in a busy town centre. This poem evokes the feeling of memories within the whispering trees which are part of the churchyard.

THE BLOSSOM TREE ON AVERY HILL

O' Frothy Delight
In pink and white
From snobbery please refrain
We know we are bare
And cannot compare
For we are still
Nature's plain
Beg pardon
Queen of April
But there is no need to gloat
For soon we will don
Our summer dress
Then blossomless
You will not impress.

by Lorraine Jones

Many Eltham streets and parks have magnificent mature flowering trees This poem describes the time when the blossom erupts in April in Avery Hill. Lorraine Jones dedicated this poem to her aunt Winifred Spinks.

1960's Eltham High Street

1917 Court Yard Eltham

Bob Hope Theatre - John King

Eltham Centre - Gaynor Wingham

CELEBRATING LIFE IN ELTHAM TODAY

WE LOVE ELTHAM!

Hot Rich coffee beans
Making me feel thirsty
Delicious doughnut smells
Dancing around me
People pushing wanting deals
Busy selling items as fast as they can
Children running up and down
Teachers shouting angrily at the children
Singing songs with my friends
Chunky books filling rusty shelves
Naughty babies taking books
Beware shh people reading
Children screams of joy
Barking dogs chase each other
My friends coming towards me
We play, I feel excited to be here

by Hannah Graham and Shannel Jackson aged 10.

This poem which is full of life and energy by Hannah and Shannel from Middle Park Primary School describe different aspects of living in Eltham .

Snapshot of Eltham by a copper

The women whose handbag was stolen
Two boys fighting, their faces swollen
An elderly man just wants a smile
Schoolgirls at the bus stop in single file
Teary eyed boy crying his dog is missing
Young lovers on a bench kissing
Little girl who can't find her mum
Lonely pensioner feeling glum
Noisy teenagers shouting on the bus
An angry shopkeeper making a fuss
The builder carrying a heavy load
The hum of traffic on the road
In the sunshine, in the grey
Today, tomorrow, any day
A snapshot of Eltham High Street
And ME, a copper, on the beat!

by Sgt Marianne Catmull

This poem won 2nd prize in the Adults Section and was written by our popular local police sergeant . The Safer Neighbourhoods Team are visible in the High Street and are an important part of everyday life in Eltham . The Judges commented , "The judges thought this was a very effective poem. It has a unique character, having been written, they presumed, by a police officer. It really is a snapshot of the life of Bobby on the beat, full of humour and , importantly, warmth for those living in Eltham that the police officer comes across on his or her daily rounds."

Cold Patrol

Winter roads are quiet
Quite a change from the Woolwich riot
Hands in my met vest, fingers in a French knot
I see members of the public, hurrying home in a trot.
Winter's roads are quiet
I spot another officer, he avoids the Mcdonalds I think he is on a diet?
Another boring day, because winters roads are quiet

by Dan Etem

Dan is on the beat in Eltham. Eltham can thankfully have its quieter times for a police officer.

WELCOME TO ELTHAM

Today in Eltham I saw a dowed homeless person
Someone gave him a £20 note also raised his spirit
Fresh minty smells dancing around me making my tummy rumble
hearing pupils texting also moaning on their phones
Welcome to Eltham

I needed 20p to buy a loaf of bread
A joyful man gave me the money
People complaining about the price of food going up
I shake my head angrily
Quickly walking home dirty dogs running everywhere.
Welcome to Eltham

Playing with my mates
Having fun there is room for everyone
Welcome to Eltham

By Jack Powell aged 10

This poem won 1st prize in the children's section. The Judges Commented: "Part of the criteria for judging the children's poems was the presence of an authentic children's voice. The judges felt this poem had a clear voice. The poem celebrates Eltham, while at the same time showing a sensitive recognition of poverty and some of the realities"

IN LIEU OF RADIO

An Aussie came to Eltham where he quickly found a sign
A house for sale that said for him, "Hey cobber, please be mine?"
He looked around and seen he found
The town had neither voice or sound.
he thought a bit then write a bit and started SEnine

by Ken Timbers

The post code for Eltham is SE9. Mark Wall is an Australian who came to live in Eltham and set up our popular magazine SEnine in 2007

Why I love Eltham by Beatrix Robinson

I like living in Eltham
It's lots and lots of fun
There's lovely parks and green spaces
to take your dog for a run

There's great cafes and restaurants
a gym and a swimming pool
and activities like tennis
dog training and football

The people are friendly
the shopkeepers are too.
If you walk to their shops
they stop and chat to you

I'm glad I live in Eltham
I think it's really great
I think that it is perfect
For me a little girl of eight

by Beatrix Robinson aged 8

This poem won 2nd prize in the children's section . The Judges commented, "This is a positive 'upbeat' poem written with a clear rhythm and structure which the poem uses effectively. The rhymes don't seem forced and the last line leaves a smile on the reader's face. Great care has been taken over this poem. time has been spent redrafting in order to craft the poem well - very impressive indeed'

Eltham is where I live

Eltham is the local town where I live not very far from Woolwich
London is our greater county council – our local borough is Greenwich
'Twas in 2012 we became royal - celebrating with much fun and glee
Honoured to be given such royal recognition for our part in history
Agreement from the Queen was given with great pump and fuss
Marking out Eltham forever – a great tribute to us

by Nadine Crawford-Piper

In 2012 Greenwich became a Royal Borough. There is a sense of pride in this for Eltham

Recession "The Dark Destroyer" versus "Battling" Eltham High Street

Recession stood there scowling, his face was black as thunder
He snarled and glared at the High Street and whispered, "Son you're going under"
Eltham took a backward step, not a hint of fear in his eyes
"It matters not what you try to do, we have the power to survive
You may have taken Allders, Woollies and the Co-op too
But we've still got M & S and Debenhams to carry the fight to you"
Recession hit back quickly, with pawn shops and closing-down sales
He laughed out loud and triumphantly cried "Austerity never fails!"
"There are other ways we can beat you; we've history on our side
We're the Royal Borough of Greenwich, so take that", Eltham quickly replied
"Henry V111 and Eltham Palace are the jewels within our crown
And with Sainsbury's and Next to help us, you're the one that's going down"
Eltham took a deep breath and swung a mighty punch
And Recession fell to the canvas; it was the end for the credit crunch.

by Mick Cohen

This poem won 3rd prize in the adults section . The Judges commented: "This poem contains a great idea and its subject is very contemporary. The judges enjoyed its wit and use of the extended metaphor - the battle between businesses and the people of Eltham against the economic crisis."

Advertising Eltham

A proper small town, a suburban hub
Tucked between London central and countryside Kent
Surprisingly full of green spaces and woods

Home to a glorious art deco Palace
And of Henry V111, he was here too!
Home to a verdant Pleasaunce. Both with moats!

Full of music - choirs, orchestras, groups
Full of sports - many and varied - all ages
Full of activities (consult SE9) and full cafes

The Eltham Centre is what it says
With college, pools, gym , library - cafe!
A good MP. It's a town to be involved in

Many churches - some handsome buildings
The odd eyesore. Fast trains to London
Buses galore. Who could want more?

A pleasant, green, energetic, friendly place
neither too rich nor too poor, neither right up or down
A good place to live - that's Eltham town.

by Lesley Pratt

Lesley has brought together many of the great attributes of Eltham as a place to live and is a good advert!

CELEBRATE ELTHAM

Eltham of Royal Greenwich
Treasures a history great
Its unique people
Have helped this to create

Henry V111's Palace, parks
And woodlands around
Something of interest
In every corner found

Wellhall's colourful Pleasaunce
The every busy Tudor Barn
Tucked behind Mottingham
The quiet and peaceful Tarn

Bob Hope's legacy
In his theatre we see
Preserved by his admirers
For you and me

Avery Hill Park fondly loved
By the students next door
From the centre of learning
There is sports and more

The High Street full of life
With stores and cafes abound
The Eltham Centre a focal point
Draws crowds from all around

We love St Mary's Centre
Welcoming and warm
A meeting place for groups
Carrying its own charm

The diverse Eltham residents
Proud of their dear town
Its positives must be nurtured
To make it renown

Celebrate Eltham
Love and peace our call
A sharing caring community
Will make it a haven for all

by Shaheen Westcombe

Shaheen Westcombe, a member of the Bangladeshi Women's Group, describes Eltham as a sharing, caring diverse community, which is a lovely description.

2012 Eltham High Street

Eltham Library - Gaynor Wingham

Eltham Palace - Damian Entwhistle

Eltham Park South in Winter - Gaynor Wingham

CELEBRATE E L T H A M

Everyone should visit its really worth a look
Lovely place to come to, you will learn more than from a book
Trees, woodlands, wildlife, parks and lots of open spaces
Historic palace, old houses a green chain walk you can easily trace
An interesting variety of restaurants and shops line the old high street
Maybe try shopping there, and no friendlier folk you could meet

by Julie Bartley

ELTHAM

By the ancient Palace
Men Dreamed, Loved, Toiled. Life flowed on.
Now as then Eltham thrives.

by Jan Bennett

Is Eltham a Hamlet?

Is Eltham a Hamlet?
An anagram or part of the smoke?
Where dear friends doth dwell
And laughter fills the spaces
Between the houses and the families
And kindness abounds.

by Godfrey Daniel

ELTHAM

Everyone loves the Eltham Palace and environmental centre too
Lovely Leisure Centre and Library too
The Tudor Barn is a true pleasure to go to
Happy as we are we enjoy the hairdressers and many more
Amazing atmosphere everywhere we go
More to do and play everyday

by Blessings Sibaveun aged 9

Eltham is celebrated in these short poems, playing with the letters and describing what it means to each poet.

Unlucky Eltham

Lonely as I pass by Eltham Palace
Scared I shiver in the chilly cold snow
Wild teens breaking shop windows
I hate Eltham
People breaking into shops
Teens shouting like helicopters
Broken glass all over concrete
I hate Eltham!
Eltham is a jungle
Eltham is a football stadium
Horrible aromas filling up my nose
I hate Eltham!

By Zainab Kadir aged 10

Eltham can be a frightening place at times. The riots in the Summer of 2011 resulted in some broken shop windows and police helicopters circling for hours overhead. This poem brings together a feeling of a cold winter, horrible smells with the fear and uncertainty of crime through a child's eyes.

ELTHAM BY BRONWYN PRITCHARD

With a Sainsburys and an Argos and a Wimpy's for lunch
Your long straight and easy high street is the best of the bunch

Avery Hill and Glenesk and many other parks scattered around
When I approach from a distance I'm excited by their sounds

You have your own Palace and leisure centre
and a new Eltham and an old for adventure

You are even in a Royal borough which gives you some class
And I can't wait 'till I'm eleven so I can explore with a new bus pass.

by Bronwyn Pritchard aged 10

This poem won 3rd prize in the children's section. The Judges commented: "Once again the judges were impressed by how the poet has carefully crafted this poem. taking time to ensure the lines work well for maximum effect. This is a positive and humorous poem which mentions many of the sights of Eltham. The poem celebrates a child's eye view in a positive and humorous way"

Eltham! Eltham! Eltham!

Eltham Eltham is lots of fun
Eltham Eltham come everyone
It's hard in Eltham even for me
I like Eltham because we have families

Eltham Eltham is lots of fun
Eltham Eltham come everyone
You can hear birds tweeting tweet, tweet, tweet
I almost want to sing with them

I look up to the sky and here I am in Eltham
It's like fairy land
Eltham Eltham is lots of fun
Eltham Eltham come everyone

by Ariona Abdullah aged 8

DEANSFIELD SCHOOL

Deansfield is a good school
Even if it is too old.

By Oscar Hicks aged 6

ELTHAM IS REALLY FUN

Monday to Friday I go to school
All the teachers are really cool
Eltham Eltham is really fun

The playground is so huge
It makes giant puddles in the afternoon
Eltham Eltham is really fun

Fridays are fun just because
These days are near the holidays
Eltham Eltham it's really fun, Saturday

Sundays are the best days of all because I have Mcdonalds and KFC!
Eltham Eltham is really fun.
Sundays is Eltham quiet and most are always at home
Eltham Eltham it's always fun .

by Cedric Sebaleke aged 8

Lots of children have fun in Eltham as can be shown in their poetry! Even if schools are old they are good.

In Praise of Eltham

I do not live in Eltham
So I suppose I am a sham
But one thing is for sure –
A fan I am.

I love its shops and restaurants
It has great Christmas lights
And of course the GAMD Choir
Which meets on Monday nights.

It has the Bob Hope Theatre
With many stylish shows
Also the Tyler theatre
Of which not everyone knows.

It has lots of parks
A swimming pool
Eltham Palace too.
So if you take a good look around
You could love Eltham too.

by Liz Davies

You don't have to live in Eltham to love it! It is a meeting place for many people who live nearby and enjoy taking part in what Eltham has to offer . Liz lives in nearby Sidcup.

Eltham Palace - Damian Entwhistle

Tarn Bridge - Michael Robinson

Pleasaunce Walk - John King

Tudor Barn - Gaynor Wingham

CELEBRATE ELTHAM

I'm glad I live in Eltham
I think it's a lovely place
when I think I live here
It puts a smile on my face

When you go up the High Street
There's everything you need
You can buy whatever you want
From some ham to a book to read

Pets Pantry, Ink and Folly
Lots of places to buy shoes
A vet, a Bob Hope Theatre
And a Farmers Market too

If you want to go out for lunch
You can go wherever you feel
Would be the perfect restaurant
For that particular meal

The Yak n Yeti or perhaps
Ziyafet is the place for you
The Eltham Grill or the Lale
Why there's another two

Everyone's very friendly
They greet you with a grin
The shopkeepers all say 'good morning'
Whenever you come in.

When you want to clear your head
And go for a nice long walk
There's so many lush green spaces
It makes you start to gawk

There's Oxleas Wood and Eltham Park
And a field of donkeys too
The Tarn and Fairy Hill Park
All under a sky of blue

For those of you that like history
We've got the Tudor Barn
It's also got a restaurant
That helps improve its charm

There's also Eltham Palace
Where Henry the V111 grew up
It's also got some lovely gardens
a tearoom and a shop

No matter what you like
Eltham's the place to be
It's the perfect place for you
and the perfect place for me.

by Hugo Robinson aged 10

A great poem which looks at all the places and activities which make living in Eltham good for Hugo aged 10 and puts a smile on his face.

8th Birthday in Eltham

Jolly classmates singing happy birthday birthday
Pumt up about today
Feeling really delighted as well
I am going to my fav place Eltham High Street.
Going to Macdonalds having fun. Feeling confident
Crispy lovely nugett smell crawling up my nose.
Eager to order
BEST PLACE EVER!

By Shukrat Adebayo aged 10.

*Children love celebrating their birthdays and having a great time in an Eltham restaurant
is clearly what Shukrat did.*

THE LIBRARY

Libraries have books like Fairy Tales
You have to be quiet
We go to Eltham Library
Sit on the rocker or Elmer Rug grab a book
And get nice and snug
You can talk but just remember
Be quiet because people are reading
You can share your book and decide
who will take it home

by Rebecca Elkins aged 5

The library in the Eltham Centre offers children a time of peace and quiet and an opportunity to explore the world of books. Rebecca at aged five was the youngest child to submit a poem and what a good poem it is.

WHERE I AM GROWING UP

Eltham is a normal place
Adventurous it can be
Where there is open space
High St, shops and people

People can be moral
all types are in Eltham
Henry V11 lived here and was royal
Past, present and future

An Eltham hubbub
Eltham Park South it is
Especially for the summer
Loads of young people go there
But just listen to the stories of the adults

By Francis Wright aged 12

Francis has written a poem of what Eltham means for him growing up here.

Eltham Poem

Eltham Palace is enchanting
As well as their splendid gardens
There's something for everyone to enjoy
A great day with so much joy.
There's marvellous panelled halls.
We all have a set of rules.
Well Hall Pleasaunce and the Tudor Barn
Like in Court road the Tarn
Eltham Lodge and Royal Blackheath Golf club
Everybody loves a big nice hug.
The Eltham Centre
Passing by Bob Hope Theatre
A Grassy Eltham Park South area
Like our great Eltham Centre
St John the Baptist Parish Church
Everyone likes a nice research
The large play area and cafe in Avery Hill Park
That's the place full of bark

by Arielle Cross aged 11

There are so many places that Arielle has told us about in Eltham she enjoys.

Dearest Eltham

The Pleasance flowers in vast array,
Attracting visitors day upon day,
Gliding gracefully down the moat serene,
Past babbling fountains and the bowling green.

Living in the Tudor Barn,
Just a stone's throw from our beloved Tarn,
Edith Nesbit, a poet herself,
Wrote The Railway Children that lines everyone's shelf.

No doubt Eltham is a lovely place,
But what really brings a smile to many a face ,
Is not the history nor the parks so near,
but the good -natured residents that live and work here.

by Katy Jebson aged 11

Eltham has a history and parks, but also good people, which Katy identifies.

ELTHAM IS MY FRIEND

For Eltham - read friend
The friend I always longed for
When I was small & unsure
The friend who came in dreams
To protect & keep me safe from all
The things life had in store

The place where heart & yearnings lie

The friend who gave me space
To run in park & field
To sing & play in summer sun
A life of friendship had begun

Like a friend it offered me
Unconditional liberty
A way to live my life
It let me be the child I was
And later how to be a wife

A place where kings have lived & loved

A place that has never let me down
Even when things have been really bleak
I never felt the need to leave
Start afresh somewhere new
I'd feel bereft & lonely in different streets

A place with acres of royal woods & trees

But just like a good friend; it's being here
That makes Eltham the place to be
It's a lovely town, a sanctuary
An oasis, a haven and home to me

by Sue Head

Lovely imagery in Sue Head's poem of Eltham as a true friend.

ELTHAM

I can do swimming in Eltham
I can do reading in Eltham
I can feel very, very safe in Eltham
Also I can feel very hungry in Eltham
I can see lovely nice buses zooming down Eltham
I can see lot of cars racing down Eltham
I can see lots of bikes in Eltham
I can see lots of lots of busy people in Eltham
I can see traffic coming this way
I can hear lots of bees buzzing all around
Also I can hear lots of children's feet.

by Mojeed Owolabi aged 8

Mojeed describes a very busy but safe Eltham.

Royal Greenwich - Jean Lendon

Journey through Eltham!

Relaxed is how I feel in my local area Eltham
I can hear people chatting on their phones
Lonely people sitting down. I am getting impatient
When is this bus coming? Fresh smells of very rich and tasty coffee

Hearing people scream and shout
Annoyed elderly people complaining about children
Men smoking making the clouds cough
Giggling people chuckling about jokes

Excited people having fun
Jumping around, running
The sun is smiling
People having ice-cream
There are some parks in Eltham so come and have some fun.

by Daniel Akpan aged 9

Daniel sees a lot going on and there is so much description and fun in this poem.

THE SNUG

The Snug opens four days a week at ten.
It is manned by Shirley, Margaret, Anna, Jen & Jen
A merry band of volunteers who look forward to greeting their customers with cheer
There is Reg and Len and also Jim who are waiting to come in
Mary and Lilly also turn up, sometimes full of woe, with a cheerful smile and a chat
  with the girls they go.
More folks arrive and there is a queue. Mine is a tea and a slice of toast too
I'll have a coffee we hear Betty say, I am off to play bowls today.
Pauline and Alan sit by the window, that pair are full of jokes.
Tea and coffee is flowing now our customers sat at tables.
New friends young and old join in with the throng. If they are lucky Reg will give
  them a song.
HELLO says Charles all suited and booted. He takes off his hat! Oh he is such a nice
  chap.
Folks are leaving one by one it's 12 o'clock and our work is done.
We hope our customers leave uplifted.
We volunteers are truly gifted!!

By Jennifer Smith

*Volunteers are the backbone of a community. The Snug is a community cafe in St Mary's
Centre in Eltham High Street with a group of dedicated volunteers providing a welcoming
cup of tea and company .*

VISIONS OF ELTHAM

Eltham
home of singers and songs
evoking thoughts of minstrels at the ancient palace.
The tilt yard inspiring visions of knights of old
brave and bold
competing for honour and glory.
These images mingle with the shoppers in the High Street
on a busy Saturday morning.
And now we are royal once more.

by Terry Timmons

*Eltham has been Royal for centuries, but the award of the title Royal Greenwich in 2012
was a source of pride and celebration in the area.*

MY HOME ELTHAM

Safely I walk out of the door with my friend
Thinking of the ground we are walking on
Henry V111 walked over it as well
I wave to my friends like the Queen
Heading to Eltham High Street
My school stands there glaring at me
I sprint with my friends to the coop
Coins jingling. excitedly I spend my money
Hopping on the bus we chat to the driver
Dreading to go home I walk to the front door.
Bye Bye

by Elizabeth Collett aged 10

Many children were very aware of the history of Eltham and the Royal connections and how they now live their lives here

Poem of Eltham

Monday to Friday I go to school
All of the teachers are so cool
The playground is so huge
It rains very often in the afternoons
Teachers teach us every lesson
It's easy to do lots of fun lessons

Monday to Friday I go to school
I like having pack lunch at school
I see most of my friends having school dinners
I like seeing the cake
I like seeing those yummy school dinners

Monday to Friday I go to school
On the weekend I go swimming too
Swimming is fun and I enjoy it too
Monday to Friday I go to school
Eltham is the best of all

by Brooke Banks aged 8

School plays a great part of children's lives and this was evident in the poems. It was good to see how much children enjoyed their school days and school was cool!

DEFINITELY ELTHAM

It's Eltham
Not Lewisham or Newham
It's Eltham
Not Birmingham or Wokingham
Definitely Eltham
Not Fulham or Tottenham
Most definitely Eltham
Nowhere near Nottingham or Manchester
This is most certainly, definitely Eltham

by Alex Wingham

It is clear from the poems that Eltham is definitely Eltham! There can be challenges but there is much to celebrate and be proud of.

Eltham Coppers - Gaynor Wingham

SEnine Magazine With Town Sign

April 2013 Eltham Poetry Competition Event. Prof Andrew Lambirth and Gaynor Wingham with staff and pupils from Middle Park Primary School

Competition Winners Middle Park School - John Webb

Olympic Torch 2012 - Eltham High Street - Gaynor Wingham